BELIEF II

by

Joseph Houston

Contents

British Library Cataloguing in Publication Data:
A catalogue record for this publication
is available from the British Library

ISBN   978-1-871828-68-9

© Joseph Houston

2009

Typeset in 11 pt Garamond
and published in 2009 by the Handsel Press
at 35 Dunbar Rd, Haddington EH41 3PJ
handsel@dial.pipex.com

Cover design and printing by
West Port Print & Design Ltd, St Andrews (01334 477135)

Thanks are expressed to the Drummond Trust
of 3 Pitt Terrace, Stirling,
for assistance with the publication of this booklet

Belief in God

The importance of the question 'Does God exist?' for our life and our society (will these be God-centred, or not?), and the pressing need to think reasonably about it makes the Theism/Atheism debate a prime topic for study in school or university. Moreover engagement in that debate enables us better to deal with other sorts of strongly felt disagreements constructively – to approach the truth together rather than come to blows.

This short book is written to help students at Advanced Religious Studies level, and others who wish to gain some grasp of some leading issues. Everything in the booklet is to be read questioningly: it is written not, of course, to lay down a view, but to help readers think well about the topics. (Scottish Advanced Higher candidates in Religious, Moral and Philosophical Studies will, in the compulsory Philosophy of Religion component, cover just the ground looked at here. The issues raised here may be more than is minimally required. However this does enable issues and arguments of interest or particular topicality to be selected for attention.)

Readers who wish to see further what the protagonists in these debates said or wrote are at an advantage because of the current availability of excellent collections of well-chosen extracts. References are made in the text of this booklet to extracts from books listed inside the back cover, and these should be studied alongside this booklet - not ignored as happens with too many longer reading lists!

Many many arguments have been, and still are, offered aiming to give reasons for believing in the existence of God (and Christians have often tried in this way to fulfil the instruction of St Peter to give a reason for the hope which is in them – see 1 Peter 3.16). Since it could take a lifetime and a library of books to give a fair treatment to all of them, we have to select.

We will begin by looking at versions of two of the 'traditional' arguments (so called without there being a clear conception of where this 'tradition' began, by whom, and for what purpose). We shall test their strengths, and where flaws are identified we shall ask whether suggested amendments, improvements or adaptations fare better. If all versions of these two arguments fail, atheism, the belief that there is no God, does not yet follow. There are several other kinds of arguments for God's existence of which some or all, so far as *our* investigations reach, may succeed.

However, there have been those who offered arguments not merely countering arguments for God but also aiming to establish the truth of atheism. Or, more modestly, they have argued that atheism is the view reasonable people should adopt or presume. We shall consider both these types of reasoning: arguments that atheism is true and arguments that it should be at least our default position.

Many notable philosophers held that there is a God. So, as reported or maybe reconstructed by Plato, Socrates, Plato (427 - 347 BC) and Aristotle (384 - 322 BC) held their theism without appeal to any revelations – inspired prophets or scriptures – on the basis of reason. Admittedly there are differences between them over exactly what God is like; but there is just enough in common between their conceptions of God and ours to justify saying that it is God they're talking about. (Some of their arguments are in the Helm collection)

The arguments which have been most discussed in the West during the last 100 years or so are those treated by Thomas Aquinas (1225 - 74) in a passage which occupies less than five pages in Helm's anthology (Helm pp.101-6). There Aquinas gives his reasons for sidelining the so-called Ontological Argument most firmly associated with Anselm, and for setting out and endorsing five other arguments for God's existence, the **Five Ways**. Of these, four deal with the basis or causes of: (i) motion or change, (ii) causes-and-effects, (iii) contingent (to be explained) things, (iv) superlative goods and perfections; the fifth aims to account for the ordered character, apparently purposive, in the sequence of events in nature. The four are customarily classed and grouped under the heading: **cosmological arguments**; and the fifth is seen as a type of argument from design, or **teleological argument** ('teleological' meaning 'having to do with purpose'). It may be that it is because this five-page passage is so brief and clear it has drawn all who wish to study arguments about God's existence to it, as a 'must read'. Certainly, the topics raised in *it* are on the agenda of anyone who studies the reasonableness of belief in God. Forced to select, we look at four of the Five Ways, omitting only the fourth.

Cosmological Arguments

So to the first three of the Five Ways. The first is presented by Aquinas, in different places, in terms either of *motion* or in terms of *change*. (See Peterson, Hasker, etc., pp.194-96 for the version in terms of movement, and Helm, pp.104-6 for the version in terms of change.) The courses of these arguments are so similar, employing near parallel moves, that it is reasonable to deal with them together to begin with. (This is so even though, as we will see, the argument when presented in terms of movement raises some problems which are avoided when the central concept is that of change.)

Below are the steps of the core argument in terms (here) of motion, to show that there is a God. Our principal purpose is to **evaluate arguments** – do they establish what they claim to establish, and if not what is it that is wrong with them? But first it is necessary to grasp exactly what they are. Aquinas does not use numbered steps expressed *just* like this; but you can check this introductory version against (the translation of) Aquinas's statement.

(1) Whatever is moved is moved by something else;

(2) Some things are in motion;

(3) Whatever is in motion, call it W, is moved by something else, call it V, that moves it;

(4) This something else V is either moved or not moved;

(5) If V is not moved, we have arrived at an unmoved mover, and that is what we call God;

(6) If V is moved, it is moved by another, call it U;

(7) Either this regress of causes goes back, W, V, U.... A..... and beyond forever, i.e. to infinity, or we must arrive at some unmoved mover;

(8) But it is impossible to regress to infinity;

(9) Therefore, we must hold that there is a first, unmoved mover, whom people call God.

Aquinas states that steps (1) and (8) stand in need of further supporting argument which he tries to supply (making some use of Aristotle's thought) to try to make his case. (For what it matters to us, i.e. not much, this first way of Aquinas is, as a whole, fairly attributable to Aristotle: see the extract in Helm, pp.24-30.)

As for step (1), *we* might be inclined to doubt it for these three reasons:

(a) We think things (clocks perhaps), animals and humans can move themselves, are *self*-movers. If we are correct in that, some things which are moved are not 'moved by something else'.

(b) According to the physics which we have learned from Newton (born 1642, so post-Aristotle and post Aquinas) bodies will continue in motion indefinitely unless acted upon by a force, so that something which has been *eternally in motion* may be in motion now without ever having *been* moved: it keeps moving along. (In his book *The Five Ways*, Routledge, 1969, A. Kenny highlights this problem.)

(c) Since movement is a *relative* notion, it is not clear whether or when something is in motion. Isn't an object's movement essentially relative to something stationary, or to some given frame of reference? Most often, in ordinary conversation we do not need to specify the assumed frame of reference because the context, the situation, makes that clear. In (1) no context is given and some sort of absolute or basic non-situated sort of movement is referred to. But isn't movement-relative-to-nothing-in-particular problematic or even a meaningless notion?

Aquinas himself discusses (a): The examples offered of so called self-movers are instances where the whole object, or person, is moved by a *part* of itself. The clock's moving comes about as some parts of the clock act to move the clock; an animal's movement is brought about by the movement of, for example, its foot. In such cases, the whole thing which is said to move does not, as that whole thing, cause itself to move: rather, *parts* act on other parts generating the so-called and misleadingly described self-movement, of the clock or the animal. And the parts which bring about the movements of these wholes are themselves acted on, are themselves moved, in order for them to act to move. So, Aquinas thinks, the cases of supposedly self-moving things do not, on due consideration, require us to reject (1).

With reference to (b), Newton's physics could not, of course, have been taken account of by Aquinas, so he cannot fairly be accused of negligence here. But our concern in these pages is not over whether Aquinas or anyone else is him-or-herself praiseworthy or blameworthy. Rather, we aim to find out whether their *arguments*, or variations or improvements on them, are sound (having true premises and proceeding by logically valid steps) so generating true conclusions. So: *does* the Newtonian point behind this issue (b) fatally undermine Aquinas's argument?

Someone might say modern cosmogony (theory about how the universe originated) rescues Aquinas. The currently favoured 'Big Bang' theory says that no moving object did in fact move without being moved, from infinitely far in the past. All movement, so the theory goes, must have started, and *been* started, at the Big Bang. Any possibility of an object's continuing in motion indefinitely, having and needing no beginning, is it seems only a possibility which is/was not made a reality, according to scientific research. Perhaps, then, Newton's conception of such an object has no relevance to present discussion? The trouble with this is said to be that if we are trying to evaluate Aquinas's argument, and so to determine whether its conclusion follows from its premisses, the fact that at step (1) he does not exclude the *possibility* of there being continuously moving objects which were never acted upon but have always moved, from eternity, means his argument can be undercut insofar as it is intended and assessed just as a piece of logically rigorous reasoning. That possibility entails that he cannot simply say, 'Whatever is moved is moved by something else.' Even if science tells us that the possibility was never made actual, still the soundness of Aquinas's argument is undermined unless some better defence against problem (b) of that argument can be found.

A better hope for defenders of Aquinas may be to insist that even if there had been a moving object which had moved unacted-upon and from a time infinitely far in the past, there would remain the question: why has this object been *moving* (for a past eternity)? It will be the fact of its motion which calls for explanation. No doubt each phase of its motion can be understood and explained in terms of a preceding phase, and that preceding phase by a phase before that, and so on, forever. But why is this object (eternally) moving at all? This eternally existing thing *might*, presumably, have been eternally at rest; so why is it, and why has it been, in motion?

A defender of Aquinas may say that if there had been an eternally moving but unacted-upon entity its movement would be unaccounted for. This defender of Aquinas can accept that in dealing with the physical world we observe – for predicting its behaviour and using it for our purposes – Newton's physics is accurate and effective; but that in order to account for the origins of that world, we need a different sort of explanation. The inadequacy of a simply Newtonian theory to explain the origin of the motion of an eternally moving thing shows the limitations of Newtonian physics. Within its limitations, it is magnificent; but it leaves an unanswered question. An answer to it may only be possible if we admit that all motion in this space-time is brought about, as (1) maintains. Since the question Aquinas is aiming to answer, in particular 'what is the origin of motion?' is left unanswerable by Newton's physics, Aquinas's attempt to answer in terms of a mover which is not part of the physical world, perhaps not in time,

7

has a rationale; it is reasonable because the attempt to rule out (1) on the Newtonian ground leaves the question unanswered.

As for (c), since everything we now see is in motion in relation to something else but at rest in relation to yet some other thing, Aquinas will have to clarify what is meant by 'moved' in (1). After all, something which was at rest in relation to the earth's surface may be set in motion relative to the earth's surface but then be at rest relative to something else – the express train which they've boarded, or the moon.

We shall return to (c) when, shortly, we see how some problems we have discovered in this argument from motion and movers are absent when the variant parallel argument in terms of change and changers is studied.

Aquinas himself saw a need to back up statement (8) of his argument (as well as (1)). In statements (6) and (7) he says that the sequence of movers can go back, and back: W, V, U.... A.... and so on. But, he says in (8), it cannot go back infinitely, to infinity. Why not? It is because in a series like this it is the first mover which 'is the cause of motion for all the others', and so if there is no first mover, all movers being intermediate movers, there will be no motion at all. There must therefore be a first mover. This first mover is what people mean by God. (Peterson, Hasker, etc., p.196)

The trouble with this argument for statement (8) is that taken in its plain meaning it just *assumes* what it needs and aims to prove. Aquinas, (as Aristotle before him, *Physics* viii, 5) claims, in statement (8), that there cannot be an infinite sequence of movers going back and back forever; and *that* is what he is now trying to demonstrate by argument, so as to convince people who might *doubt* it, or not see good reason for agreeing with it. He then tells us that if there is no first mover to start movement, there can be no subsequent or intermediate movers, no movers at all. But if an infinite going-back of movers *is* possible, as the people who doubt (8) suspect, there *can* perfectly well be many movers in sequence(s) without any first mover, because an infinite sequence does go back forever and ever *without* there being or having to be any first member. It is only if we can *assume* or have a *basis* for the impossibility of an infinite series of movers that Aquinas's assertion 'without a first in the series of movers there will be no movers at all' can seem to be true and have force here. However, if there are doubts about the impossibility of an infinite regress or if someone rather suspends judgement about (8) what Aquinas apparently argues should have no force at all to remove the doubt about, or secure assent to, (8). We have not been given an independent reason, a reason independent of itself, to think (8) is true.

(In *assuming* the very statement which is in question, in order to support it, Aquinas is guilty of the fallacy of *begging the question*. This kind of flaw in an argument has to be distinguished from raising or inviting a question. People, especially journalists, often talk about some event or comment as 'begging the question' of such-and-such, when what they mean is that it prompts or leaves unanswered the question of such and such. But this is a recent (and loose?) usage. Begging the question is more properly or strictly a failure and a fallacy in *arguing*. It is assuming something, or the very thing, which is in dispute. If you assume *it* when it is the statement you are trying to confirm or defend, then you have failed, as Aquinas appears to have failed here.)

Could Aquinas have provided a good reason for people who need to be convinced of it, to accept (8)? Two possible reasons can be considered:

(i) There is a type of cosmological argument which was put forward by Islamic thinkers and is called Kalam cosmological argument. We'll look at this later. These thinkers gave their reasons for rejecting the possibility of there being a real infinite – an actual series of events, an actual period of time or expanse of space which was or is infinite. While the *idea* of an infinite may be of use in mathematical speculation or reasoning, they held that actual infinities raise such paradoxical implications that reasonable people will recognise that no real infinity is possible. (Some modern mathematicians such as Hilbert (1862 - 1943) agree with them.) One such paradox is this: suppose a planet takes ten years of our time to go round its sun, while a moon of that planet goes round the planet five times in a year of our time: so in the time it takes for the planet to make one revolution of its sun, the moon will have completed 50 revolutions of its planet. If these bodies have existed in their stable system for an infinite time they will have completed the *same* number of revolutions, an infinity.

If we think, with the Kalam writers, that it is more reasonable to deny real infinities than accept conclusions like that about the planet and the moon, we may have located a reason which Aquinas could have used to defend his (8). (It seems likely that Aquinas knew the Kalam argument but chose not to use it.)

(ii) Aquinas might have argued that to suppose there might have been an infinite regression would leave the whole infinite series **without an explanation**, or reason. And, indeed, perhaps each mover in an unaccounted-for sequence of movers is only partially and not completely accounted for unless the series is explained? All this, which 'Aquinas might have argued' has been denied, notably by Bertrand Russell; we must look at what he said and consider possible replies (if any) on behalf of Aquinas.

Russell maintained (as others have done) that if there is an infinite series of movers, or changers, or causers each acted on by a predecessor in the series, a series having no beginning, then each item in this series is explained by the action of its predecessor(s). And if each member of the sequence is accounted for, explained, in that way, so is the whole series. There is no place or need for any other sort of explanation of the whole series (Russell pp.15-16). These claims seem perhaps most convincing in relation to the First Cause argument (The Second Way of Aquinas, which follows the pattern of the series (1) – (8), modified to speak of causation rather than motion). If there is a causal series, where each thing is causally accounted for by a preceding thing or preceding things, and where there are infinitely many things going back to infinity it *looks* as if we have an explanation for the existence of the whole series. But if we think about motion again, the Russell claim does not perhaps *seem* so forceful: suppose each moved item is moved by (a) predecessor(s) and the sequence of moved movers goes back forever, we have an explanation for the motion of each thing. But we do *not* have an explanation for there being any motion at all. Why is this infinite number of items in a sequence where there's *motion?* Why is there not rest rather than motion? Similar points apply to the argument from change. And, returning to the First Cause argument, why, in the infinite series of causes supposed by Russell, is any causing going on? The idea that in an infinite regression of movers (or changers or causes) the series is as a whole fully explained when and because each item is explained, is now unconvincing, because the very fact of motion (or of change or of causal action) will be unexplained.

If we explicitly add the statement that the motion, change, and causing must *have* an explanation to the conclusion we just reached – that if there has been an infinite regress of movers/changers/causers, there is *no* explanation of motion, change or causing – we reach Aquinas's (8): an infinite regress is impossible. Whether or not this is what Aquinas had in mind, it is an argument for (8) which he or his supporters might offer.

The statement which was explicitly added, that there must be an explanation, a reason, for motion etc., may be implicit in Aquinas. The statement is a form of the **Principle of Sufficient Reason** which has been employed and defended, in rather the way just exemplified, by many authors. For a recent use and defence of it, see also the introductory book *Metaphysics* Chapter 7 by Richard Taylor.

Aquinas gives a formulation of his First Way in terms of change as well as in terms of movement; and of course it looks very like the earlier (1) – (9). So he begins by saying that whatever is in process of change must be changed by something else (see Helm p.105), goes on to affirm that some things *are* in process of change, and pursues his reasoning by steps closely analogous to those of the argument about motion. Still there are differences between the two courses of reasoning (because change is not quite the same as motion).

Where the new statement (1) reads, as it does, 'anything in process of change is being changed by something else', likely objections occur to Aquinas, objections which are analogous to those addressed already in connection with (1) as it considers motion. Why, then can something not change of itself; why must it be changed *by another*? Aquinas says that change is a process of moving from an actual condition to a condition which was only a potential condition for that thing; and something can only be moved from being potentially x to being actually x by something which is/has x itself. The example he gives in this: 'fire which is actually hot, causes wood, which is able to be hot, to become actually hot, and in this way cause change in the wood.' (see Helm, p.105). Something which is able to change to being y is *only* potentially y, and change requires to be effected by something which is actually y, has y itself; nothing can effect change in and of itself. In this way, Aquinas defends his (1) as it applies to change. Questions we might raise could point out seeming counter-examples: rubbing two sticks together can make both hot even though neither stick, nor the person or machine doing the rubbing is hot; the smell of cooking bacon may change you into a hungry person although the smell is not in itself hungry.

The Newtonian possibility of an unacted-upon eternally moving object may be relevant *here*: motion is a type of change, change of position. That possibility undermines Aquinas's (1) in relation to change because it says that something could change continuously from eternity *without* being changed. Agreed that it may not change itself; but it is not changed (as Aquinas says it must be) by another. One reply on behalf of Aquinas is predictable in view of the earlier discussion about motion: A Newtonian eternally moving object will lack an explanation unless we postulate a reason for its motion which does not precede it in time, and is not actually in time at all. And on that conception it *is* or *was* acted on. So also for change. (The Principle of Sufficient Reason says, consistently with that, that there has to be a reason for its motion; and if we *cannot* have one we are justified in doubting whether the Newtonian eternal mover can exist.) A second reply on behalf of Aquinas may question whether an eternally moving, eternally unacted upon object *does* change. Does something which just keeps going as always *change* in a relevantly significant way? It changes position in relation to other things, no doubt. But you and I are changing all the time in relation to, say, the planet Jupiter: does that entail that we are *really changing* in any way that matters?

Statement (8) in respect of change, rather than motion, is defended by Aquinas, taking steps analogous to those we saw in relation to motion: there is a similar reason for accusing him of question-begging over his elimination of infinite regression. There is also the argument worth considering in favour of

11

Aquinas, whereby the Principle of Sufficient Reason permits him to rule out an infinite regress on the ground that *change* (as previously motion) will be unaccounted for if an infinite regress is treated as the complete truth.

We have now given attention to the two versions which Aquinas leaves us of his First Way, those in terms of motion and change. Moving on to his **Second Way**, we find another argument similar to our (1) – (9) but employing *causation* as the vital concept (instead of motion or change). So its first steps say:

(1) If something is caused, it is caused by something else;

(2) In the observable world, everything is caused; and the argument continues by analogy with the earlier (1) – (9) sequences.

The issues which this Second Way raises are in some cases closely analogous to issues we have already looked at. Aquinas himself tries to justify the new (1) and the new (8). Thus he holds (to support (1)) that any cause must *precede*, that is it must exist before whatever it causes, i.e. its effect. But nothing can precede itself; so nothing can be its own cause. And since everything apparently requires a cause, everything must be caused by something else. As for the new (8), he argues against an infinite going-back of causes in a series in the same fashion, adapted to a causal argument, as for motion and change. If what he says is open to the charge of being question-begging, as it seems to be, the impossibility of an infinite regress – because it will be incomprehensible in lacking an explanation of causing's going on – may be an arguable defence. The acceptability or otherwise of a Principle of Sufficient Reason will determine the strength of such a defence, as in the previous cases.

In addition to these issues, his appealing to causation has prompted further distinct objections directed at this Second Way. Notably Hume (1711-76) and his many admirers such as Russell (1872 - 1970) or Dawkins (1941 -) have asked whether each thing (events or 'things', meaning objects) *must* have a cause. We do habitually observe events to occur in accordance with recurring patterns of sequence: the sun shines and the flowers open, rabbits copulate and multiply, the sculptor sculpts and a statue emerges. (Of course, we come to differentiate between mere recurring sequence and causation: the school bell rings and the children cascade from school but are not exactly *caused* to by the bell.) But if this attribution of causation is *only* a matter of our habit in perception, as arguably it may be, *need* events or things actually have causes? Maybe, sometimes there may be uncaused events and things? We seem to be able to imagine such a possibility at least. Perhaps one of the moons of Saturn just popped (or slowly emerged) into existence without any cause? Hume has seemed to say that a test for whether something is possible is that we can imagine it: if we can imagine it, it is possible. So if we can imagine an uncaused something-or-other, as it seems that we can, it is *not* necessary that every entity should have, or have had, a cause; and, in that case Aquinas's step (2) about causation is open to question, and should not be depended on. If all this is correct the Second Way cannot be relied upon either.

However, there is a good deal to question in this Hume-following reasoning. First, the imaginative powers of particular people do not, surely, provide a trustworthy test of what is really possible, or not, out there in the world? The imaginative powers of people vary: whose should we trust for guidance? Why indeed should *any* human imagination be supposed to give reliable guidance on this? Second, it seems obvious that in fact there are all kinds of events which we can imagine (quite easily) while not taking at all seriously any idea that they could actually occur: a frog turns into a prince, or vice versa; the fairy-godmother creates a carriage (and carriage horses) from nothing, with a wand-wave: and so on. In fact, an adult who seriously thinks such things are (even) possibilities will be thought disordered in mind. Accordingly, if we are, as we surely are, disposed to seek out causes of facts and events and things, Hume-type reasonings do not call for us or Aquinas to change that disposition. Causes *are* to be sought out.

A recurring objection is raised against one, or another, or all of these three courses of reasoning, from motion, change and cause. Against each the accusation has been that the conclusion is inconsistent with a principal premiss. Take the argument from motion: the objection is that the first and unmoved mover (obviously) moves, according to Aquinas's reasoning. Yet the first statement amounts to saying that whatever moves is moved by another. So it seems to follow that the first mover must be moved by another, in which case it is not unmoved. The conclusion of the reasoning (1) to (9) is inconsistent with its starting point; the whole reasoning of this first way is, allegedly, incoherent.

The objection, common as it is, arises from a careless reading of what Aquinas says together with a failure to recognise an ambiguity in the use of the word 'mover'. On this latter point, 'mover' can mean 'bringing movement about', or on the other hand, 'being in motion'. The prime mover is a mover in the former way: it brings movement about. But it does not follow that it is itself in motion. (We may tend to conceive of the sequence of moves rather as a series of billiard balls each of which moves because a previous ball in the sequence collides with it imparting (some of) *its* motion to the ball which is moved. If that is our picture, of course any imparter of motion, any mover, *will* be pictured as being itself in motion. For Aquinas, though, the prime mover imparts motion without itself being in motion.) Not only is it not in motion but it is not moved.

Aquinas says in (1) that only what *is moved* is moved by another. Aquinas does not say that the first mover is moved; and the first mover only moves in the sense of moving something else. So there is no problem of squaring what he says about the First Mover with what he says about things which are moved and so are in motion: only these latter have to be moved by another. (Check Aquinas's words in Helm and in Peterson, Hasker, etc.)

Rather similar responses can be made to the similar objections that there's internal inconsistency between what is said respectively about all which changes, and all which causes, and the First Source of Change and the First Cause. Briefly touching on the last of these: Aquinas is accused of saying that everything must *have* a cause and yet concluding that there must be a First and *uncaused* Cause. This would be inconsistent, and would call for the common question 'Who made, caused, God?' But Aquinas only says that we do not and cannot *observe* anything causing itself; the things we experience are caused by something else, but God is not: the First Cause is uncaused. Aquinas's principle is not that *everything* must have a cause, but that the sequence of causes 'must stop somewhere'. There is no inconsistency there, inviting the question 'Who made God?' (The series must stop somewhere because an infinite regression will leave the fact of there being a causal series unexplained.)

Of course, even if careful reading of what Aquinas said reveals some common objections to the first two Ways to be lacking force, there may well be other more serious problems for him.

We must turn, now to the Third Way. This focuses on a distinction between what need not exist, on the one hand, and what must exist, on the other. Often the distinction is expressed as being between: (a) contingent beings (which need not exist or need not have existed) such as cabbages and kings, suns and books, all which as Aquinas says 'we find ...... springing up and dying away, thus sometimes in being and sometimes not.' (Helm, p.105), and (b) necessary beings,' such things as must exist. According to Aquinas it is not possible that everything can be, or have been, contingent. That is because something which *need* not exist must at some time have *been* non-existent, 'and if everything need not be, once upon a time there was nothing. But if that were true there would be nothing even now, because something that does not exist can only be brought into being by something already existing. So that if nothing was in being nothing could be brought into being, and nothing would be in being now, which contradicts observation. Not everything therefore is the sort of thing that need not be; there has got to be something that must be.' (Helm, p.105)

Aquinas goes on; but let us pause to digest and consider. In fact the major controversies about the Third Way are concerned with the above train of reasoning. All of these assertions, steps in Aquinas's reasoning, appear questionable and certainly have been questioned:

(i) Something which need not exist must at some time have been non-existent;

(ii) If everything need not exist, once upon a time there was nothing;

(iii) Something that does not exist can only be brought into being by something already existing.

Aquinas wants us to suppose, to see where that supposition gets us, that everything might have been or might be, contingent. Well, he says, in that case nothing would exist now; and that is obviously false. So the supposition that everything is contingent must be false. But, we want to know, *why* would nothing exist now if everything has been contingent? The answer is that something which need not be, must at some time have been non-existent, and if everything were to have been like that then at some one time there would have been nothing; and so there would be nothing now.

Take (i) though: Why should something which *need* not exist actually non-exist at some time? Perhaps, although such a thing *might* not have existed at some time, it actually always *does* exist. To take other instances: pretty obviously, although a person might not *have* to live on the Island of Islay and might not *have* to speak any Gaelic it will *not* follow that at some time she must actually have lived elsewhere or spoken some other tongue. What is not a *necessity* may possibly still always actually be the case. That is the problem for (i). What about (ii)?

(ii) depends on (i) because if some contingent thing might in fact *have* existed permanently there would always be something, namely that thing. The further problem for (ii) is over why, even if we ignore the problem facing (i), and accept it for the moment, there is no reason given why all these non-necessary, i.e. contingent, things should fail to exist *at once*. Aquinas's opponent might say that over the long aeons of time before all contingent things have gone out of existence new contingent things always come into existence. So, existence-in-things is passed on, like the baton in a relay race, from one lot of contingent things to another. *Why* may that not be the truth? Aquinas is held not to have given us any reason for (ii) either, even if (i) is treated as acceptable – and as we have seen, it too is at least problematic.

The role of (iii) in Aquinas's reasoning is to block this idea which someone might suggest: 'Perhaps into the void, such as the absence of any existing thing, when any contingent beings there have been have ceased – into this void a new contingent entity *might* simply emerge, from nothing. If that is possible, then it will not follow that if there once was nothing there would have to be nothing now. If contingent entities might pop into existence from nothing, the existing things we know now may derive from some such entity whose emergence just

15

happened. Accordingly it does not follow that because there is something now, a necessary being exists.' Aquinas's (iii) insists that no such spontaneous, uncaused emergence of an existing thing is possible.

As we saw in connection with Aquinas's Second Way (focussed on causation), the thought expressed by (iii) has been challenged, by Hume and, e.g. Russell; and in discussing these Hume-type objections to the Second Way, we looked at arguments which are the relevant arguments here. *Can* we reasonably suppose that there are uncaused entities?

There is a species of cosmological argument which was developed by Islamic thinkers such as Al-Kindi (see Helm pp.118-122) and is defended now by, for example W.L.Craig (see Peterson, Hasker, etc., pp.210-222). These **Kalam** cosmological arguments – *Kalam* means 'having respect for theological, Koranic input' – are nevertheless intended to stand up philosophically.

They begin with the issue familiar to us now of whether the universe could have had an infinite past, no beginning, no need for a First Mover, changer, cause, necessary being, or creator. Kalam arguments for a creator contended that an *actual* infinity of any sort is impossible. The *idea* of an infinity can have its uses, as an idea, helpful, maybe, in mathematical theorizing. But the Kalam thinkers argued that an actual infinity, of physical particles or periods of time, for example, is not possible. We shall see in a moment what their arguments were and are for this. First, the use they made of this conclusion should be indicated: They held that if the universe cannot have existed for an infinite time, it must have had a beginning; nothing happens without a cause, so the beginning of the universe must have had a cause. If we ask why the universe began *when* it did, an answer wholly in terms of physical conditions which existed 'prior' to the beginning is inadequate because these physical causes will surely belong in the universe whose beginning is to be accounted for. To explain the beginning and the time of it we need to invoke a cause which has a free will – and we should surely say there 'who has a free will', because only personal beings can have a will.

Having seen what is made of it, how the argument goes on, we return now to its distinctive starting step: that a real infinity is impossible. The Kalam reasoning is that if we suppose that there *are* real infinities we find that we are thereby committed to absurdities. To avoid the absurdities, we must avoid holding that there are real infinities. So what are the absurdities? One from the ancient world asks us to think of two objects in the heavens: the first, a planet, takes five years (as measured in our time) to complete one revolution of its sun; the second, a moon, completes twenty revolutions of its planet in one year, and it is therefore doing 100 times as many revolutions in unit time as the first object.

If these objects were to continue in this way for an infinite time, though, both will complete the *same* number of revolutions, that is, an infinity of revolutions.

Or imagine a library, having an infinite number of books, in which every second book is black and every other book is red. This library, then, contains an infinite number of black books and an infinite number of red books. So if you remove all the red books, the library is still the same size; there are as many red books as there are red and black books together. And if one of these books has an infinite number of pages, then if you finished reading it you'd have read the same number of pages as there are in all the infinite number of books in this infinite library.

Russell, and David Hilbert (1862 - 1943) the great mathematician both added examples of paradoxes of infinity. Hilbert's asks us to think of an hotel with an infinite number of rooms; and all the rooms are full. A new guest arrives looking for a room. Although all the rooms are full, the new guest is able to be given a room, no problem. The manager moves the person in room 1, to room 2, the person in room 2 to room 3, the person in room 3 to room 4, and so on. The new guest then moves into room 1. With the arrival of this new guest there are still the same number of guests in the hotel as before. And suppose, further, that an infinite number of new guests appear they can be fitted in also. The manager moves each existing guest into the room with the number twice his existing room (from 1 to 2, from 2 to 4, from 3 to 6 and so on) this making all the odd numbered rooms available, in his previously full hotel, for the infinity of newcomers. More paradoxes are generated by Hilbert's hotel. (See Peterson, Hasker, etc. pp.211-2).

These paradoxes are said to show that there can be no actual infinities – of objects, times, or anything else. Granted that mathematicians do talk about, and have a use for the ideas of infinity or infinities, in their reasoning; that does not entail that there is or can be anything in the actual world corresponding to this talk of the mathematicians. Recall that mathematicians have developed differing geometries: there is the geometry developed from Euclid (around 300 BC) which is what most of us start with when we work on geometry at school. But two other consistent geometries have been developed much more recently. It seems, from what modern physics tells us that Euclid's geometry does not describe our actual, real space accurately. Certainly, since they're different (e.g. over whether a straight line *is* the shortest distance between two points), all three cannot be accurate descriptions of real space; and it is possible that none of them is. Hence, from the fact that mathematicians construct particular coherent bodies of mathematical theory, in particular, here, about infinity, it does not follow that there *is* anything in the actual world to which they apply – actual infinities.

The paradoxes of infinity indicate that real infinities are, in fact, impossible; that being so, the first major step in Kalam cosmological argument is established. (Also, as remarked in our discussion of Aquinas, a line of defence for him may be available as he tries to eliminate the possibility of an infinite regression, in the course of his first three Ways: the line of defence will support his several statements (8).) The course of the argument from that first major step is given above, five paragraphs ago.

During the twentieth century, cosmology and cosmogony took account especially of work by Einstein and Hubble so that a 'Standard Model' or theory of the Big Bang has come to be most widely accepted. This is not the place to try to discuss the merits of this theory as compared to alternatives which have been on offer – such as a steady-state theory. Stephen Hawking said in 1996, and thinking of scientifically competent people, 'Almost everyone now believes that the universe and time itself, had a beginning at the Big Bang.' Where does this recent science lead us in our assessment of cosmological arguments for God's existence?

Perhaps most obviously, it seems to give good scientific reason to exclude belief in an infinite regress going back and back into an infinite past history of the universe. And, as also claimed in Kalam arguments, where a somewhat personal explanation in terms of a free will is the only possibility for explanation of the origin of the universe, so here there can be no physical conditions which explain the Big Bang, since such conditions would be part of the universe to be explained; and in addition, since the Big Bang is the beginning of time itself there is no *before* in which physical conditions could be accommodated. A contemporaneous or a timeless free will at work provides the needed explanation.

The physicist **Paul Davies** has asserted that there may well have been a probability that out of nothing there would have emerged the space-time of our universe. He has been criticised on the ground that there can be no probability of anything in particular (no probability that this will happen rather than that) in circumstances where there is *nothing*. Probabilities have to be relative to something that exists. (See W.L. Craig in Helm, pp.280ff, for the criticism of Davies.)

Those of us who are not competent physicists will be aware that in discussing these topics a cautious tentativeness is more than usually called for. Have we really understood the (often extraordinary-seeming) things which the scientists say?

One of the most puzzling issues concerns time, and its beginning. The philosopher **Kant** (1724 – 1804) argued that it cannot make sense to think that there could be a beginning of the history of the universe in time. This is one of his objections to cosmological arguments attempting to show that the universe does have a beginning in time – which is brought about by a first mover, or changer, or cause. Kant held that if we suppose some particular point to be the beginning, it will always make sense to ask what, if anything, was happening before that point. Even if there was then nothing of physical or mental reality, the empty, eventless time would still be continuous with the time after which things exist and events happen; it would still, in that way, be part of the universe. And there is a problem, further, over the idea of a beginning *of* time: The concept of a beginning of something implies that there is a time series in place, pre-existing whatever might have a beginning. 'When did the smell begin?' implies that there is and has been at least a period of time *within* which the smell began. But if we ask or talk about the beginning of time itself what time series can we be implying is in place, within which *time* began. Do we mean that there is, somehow, a time series behind, or preceding this time series? Surely not. There is one time or time within which everything happens, isn't there? Perhaps talk of a, or the, beginning of time is confused. It is certainly puzzling. Kant thought that the problem reveals our minds' inability to deal with issues about the origins of the Universe. Modern cosmogonists talk of the beginning of time, evidently making sense to one another, at least. For the rest of us an attitude of respectful humility, and an openness to learn, are in order.

Arguments from Design

The fifth of the five 'Ways' of Aquinas is reckoned to be a form of argument from design for the existence of God. Aquinas says that in all bodies obeying natural laws we see an ordered-ness, to an end. By an 'end' here he means more than a conclusion, a stopping place. He means a goal, as when people have an end, a purpose, in view. 'They truly tend to a goal, and do not merely hit it by accident.' (See Helm, p.206) The Greek word *telos* means an end, goal; so arguments from Design tend to be classed as 'Teleological Arguments'. This classification is given because each of this group of arguments claims to arrive at the existence of a purposive intelligence, with some sort of aim or end, as the explanation of what we commonly observe in nature.

What does Aquinas mean by 'tending towards a goal'? He cannot be thinking of a goal, for bodies which obey natural law, such as 'to prevent a river flooding', or 'to reward or punish an individual person'. He cannot be thinking this because we usually *cannot* see what particular immediate end, if any at all, might be being aimed for, what purpose of that particular sort is being pursued as nature takes its law-governed course.

Arguably what Aquinas means is that if, for instance, an object falls in the predictable way according to gravity-law, or water freezes in the law-like way at 0°c, the orderedness of what we see can only be explained in terms of the action of someone 'with awareness', of a purposive kind. So he is arguing for the recurrent patterns of sequence among events (objects *fall* to the ground when support is removed; water sufficiently cooled will *then* freeze); and he holds that this recurrence, this law-conforming regularity in all sequences of events in nature requires to be explained by appealing to an aware orderer of a kind which has a purpose. He might say that although a chaos, in which no natural law is known and no predictable patterns recur, is just about conceivable, we do not inhabit such a chaos. The relatively ordered world which we know, and of which science tells us more, is to be accounted for thus: 'Everything in nature, therefore, is directed to its goal by someone with intelligence, and this we call "God".' (Helm, p.106) We say this, presumably, not because we can see what the purpose is (or the purposes are) in further detail. It is rather that the only sort of explanation of this order in nature is that it is due to the sort of being which has intelligence and purpose.

Richard Swinburne offers and defends an argument which is at least similar to (this interpretation of) Aquinas's fifth Way in that it takes as its starting point the order of succession of events in time. (See Swinburne: in Helm pp.342-346, and in Davies pp.274-285; also Swinburne's own *Is there a God?* especially chapters 2 and 4.) We will discuss this Aquinas/ Swinburne argument carefully and in a moment. But first it will help if we notice that there is a distinctly different argument from design (with which we will deal later) which should not be confused with the Aquinas/ Swinburne reasoning. This other argument appeals to order in the world of a kind quite different from that which gives Aquinas/Swinburne its first step. This other order is seen in, for instance, a cleverly devised piece of machinery (for example a car engine, or, to take the standard example, a watch). What we have there is an arrangement of component parts related and interacting in ways which function usefully. It is this arrangement – together, so as to work together, of the parts of a functioning machine (like a railway engine) or system (like a heating system) which is being identified in this sort of order, which Swinburne calls the order of co-presence.

Famously, Paley (see Helm pp.189-191) imagines someone finding a watch on a moorland. (He is thinking of watches with springs, cog-wheels and so on, rather than (modern) quartz watches where there's little machinery to see; and he is thinking of a, to us, heavy pocket watch, not a wrist watch.) What do we find? 'We perceive .... that its several parts are framed and put together for a purpose.....' It was this sort of order, of co-presence, the presence together of the parts of functioning arrangements which was appealed to by people arguing from design in the 18th and 19th centuries. (Paley's book was written in 1802.) These writers saw their favoured examples in nature, especially biology: in the arrangement of the parts of animals' anatomy and physiology, in the human eye, in the ordered functioning system of a tree or a leaf. They argued that such order requires us to believe that these systems, displaying order like that, must have had an intelligent designer. Authors who advocate evolutionary accounts are, of course, advancing an alternative explanation for the emergence of this order of co-presence. (It is probably because there had been a wide appeal, even a reliance, on arguments from design resting on this order of *co-presence* that so many believers in God have wanted to argue vigorously against evolutionary ideas, and many evolutionary biologists have seemed to suppose that if *they* can show arguments from co-presence type design to be undercut, they have effectively undercut *any* belief in God. We shall take these matters up in due course.)

Back to Aquinas, Swinburne, and arguments from the order of succession among events to the existence of God: Aquinas's development of his reasoning is so brief that we are better to take up Swinburne's reasoning for our scrutiny.

Having pointed out this fact about the world: that events generally occur not in unpatterned random ways but in regular sequences, in recurrent patterns which allow us often to predict what will happen, and many of which are discovered by science – how can we *explain* this fact of the world's being an ordered cosmos and not a chaos?

Swinburne says that there are two possible kinds of explanation of some fact or event. First, it can have a *scientific* explanation, in which case we explain it as being an instance of some general pattern by which events of those sorts always follow one another. Take the case of the breaking of an apple's attachment to its tree whereupon it falls to the ground with a particular velocity. That has been given a scientific explanation which means that we show it to be an instance of what always happens when two masses (such as an apple and its planet) are close to each other: there's an attractive force between them (proportional to the product of their masses and inversely proportional to the square of the distance between them). The general rule which applies to apples and planets applies to moons and planets and all other physical entities. Another case: Railway lines tend to buckle in hot weather. Why? Because *all* metals expand when heated: in hot weather, railway lines expand and push against each other so that they buckle when the heat is great enough. That is scientific explanation. The world might not have been ordered in this way; it might conceivably have been a chaos. But it isn't a chaos; the orderedness in the sequence of events opens the way to scientific explanations (and makes purposive action by us possible because we can predict what will happen next if we do so and so).

Secondly, a fact or event can have a *personal* explanation. That will refer to the free action of a free (personal) will. Why are you reading this? Because you (exercising your free will) have chosen to do so (and chosen to stick at it). Being a *free* choice this choosing and doing is not explained in a scientific way as falling under some recurring pattern of events. Why did the car suddenly stop? Because its driver freely decided to stop. A complete explanation would involve scientific aspects e.g. about how brakes generally work; but the basic explanation is the sort of *personal* one which Swinburne is talking about.

The fact to which Swinburne is drawing our attention and which requires an explanation is the fact that events in the world take place in regular patterned sequences. Why should *this* be? It cannot be explained scientifically; a scientific explanation produces some generally observed pattern in the sequences of events and then points out that the fact to be explained fits that pattern. But if we want to know why there *are* any such patterns of regularity it will not help for an answer now to point to some very widely, generally found and exemplified regularity and say, by way of attempted explanation, that the world fits *that* pattern. Of course there would be the problem of thinking what that widely embracing pattern can be. But the more fundamental difficulty is that what we want to know is: why are there any such patterns? (If you try to explain some such patterns as instances of others, or of another, you still haven't explained why there are any such patterns, why the world is ordered in that way at all.)

It may help to consider a particular pattern of regularity, say this one about the change of state of water to ice: 'When water is cooled to 0° c, it solidifies'. How is that pattern to be explained? Well, if may fall under some general rule or pattern with a wider reference than only to water, and to circumstances surrounding change of state from liquid to solid. That may deal with alcohol, mercury, and all other liquids as well as water and have to do with the energy in the molecules of a substance (when they have so much energy that they vapourise or so little as not to remain liquid but solidify together). In turn the truth of that generalization may be explained by showing it to be covered by a general pattern wider still. But if what we want is an explanation of why the widest possible general pattern exists (which would be a way of explaining why there are any regularities at all), we cannot go any wider, to offer an explanation of *that* in terms of a wider pattern. We have to explain there being any regularities whatever in some *other* way than by looking for a wider regular pattern which it fits.

The only other sort of explanation available is a personal explanation in terms of an intelligent, freely willed choice and action. So should we accept that as an answer to our question? We do know many examples where a will and a purpose allied with intelligence brings about sequences of events, each sequence following a regularly recurrent pattern. Say a pack of cards is dealt (e.g. by a conjuror) again and again in the same sequence. Or a commuter nearly daily takes the same 15 minute short route through his housing estate to the railway station. Or a speaker much in demand at Burns Nights recites 'To a Haggis' again and again, the same sounds (words) in the same sequence every time.

The alternative to offering that sort of explanation of the world's order (of succession in time) is of being content with treating the world's ordered character as just a brute fact, needing no explanation. The world is just like that. This attitude would be treated in relation to other questions (why do swallows migrate to and from warm places? Why does the sun shine? Why do we find sunsets beautiful?) as a blameworthy refusal to try to understand. Where would we be if people had responded with 'It just is that way' to questions? Why does the tide come and go? Why is there blood in us? We call a refusal to look for an answer 'obscurantism', a bad thing.

Swinburne adds that it is a simpler, more economical explanation of the regularities in the world's sequences of events to postulate a *single* intelligent, aware orderer than to postulate more than one. This intelligent orderer must be immensely powerful and active all the time, controlling all events so that they occur in the patterns which we call laws of nature.

Many laws of nature are describable in mathematical terms of, as it seems to us, great subtlety and telling simplicity. So, to be able to order the world as we find it to be this designer must have both great power and great intelligence.

We have to beware of attributing too much to this sort of design argument. It can only claim to argue for an orderer which/who is continually present and active in the sequences of events comprising the physical world. This being will have to possess great intelligence and power. But this comes short (by some distance) of the God of the major religious traditions. The argument from design we have been considering has nothing to say about whether the ordering intelligence is good, or loving, all-knowing, having purposes for people such as renewal, salvation or sanctity. Still less does it specify particular roles in history for a race, or a particular striking individual, or a notable prophet. Like the others of the Five Ways, this argument does not establish much of e.g. Jewish, or Christian, Islamic or Hindu belief.

The strength of the reasoning in the argument depends (among other things) on the strength of the analogy at its heart. That is the analogy between on the one hand the pattern of order we see in nature, in the successions of events in time, and on the other hand the order of succession among events which we know to have been brought about by human intelligent activity. Analogies are never, and can never be, 'perfect': the word 'analogy' speaks of significant likenesses, parallels, a number of shared properties, while acknowledging differences. If there are *no* differences (or none that matter) we speak not of analogy but of complete likeness or qualitative identity. Analogies are always more or less close analogies, *short* of qualitative identity (being identically alike), so, strictly, 'perfect analogy' is a confused expression.

The main point now is that the strength of an argument based on analogy will be determined by the strength of the analogy. A weak analogy, one where the similarities are not close at very many points, will give at best only a weak argument, that is an argument which confers only a *small* probability to its conclusion. So how strong/close is the analogy at the core of this design argument? And how strong as a consequence is the argument itself? It is clear at least that this is a matter of degree. So the conclusion of the argument, namely that there is an intelligent designer whose activity orders the physical world, making it law-conforming can only be given a *degree* of probability. If the analogy is close the probability will be higher: if the analogy is less close the conclusion's probability will be less. Argument from analogy cannot give us the kind of strong proof which, it is thought, mathematics provides, where premises we cannot doubt, premises which are obviously certain truths, lead by valid reasoning to equally certain conclusions. Sometimes these are called 'knock-down' proofs. The design argument is not a proof like that. Often people seem to want, or demand, knock-down proofs in support of beliefs about God. Perhaps they long for certainty because the issues involved are so important, and the way they live their lives will be shaped by what they believe about God. (There *have* been attempts made to provide such a knock-down proof of God's existence, in the so-called Ontological Argument. We cannot give it proper attention now.) Our present concern is to say, firstly, that design arguments based on analogy are not knock-down proofs; but then to point out that very few of our beliefs are, or can be, supported by proofs of that kind. At least *theoretical* doubt is almost always possible over our beliefs: you believe that you are reading words which are on a page. But people *can* be mistaken in remembering even such things as: which combinations of letters form words, or even which shapes are letters. And our senses *can* play us tricks, e.g. maybe over whether it *is* a page that is in front of you.

Whether there was a battle at Bannockburn in 1314 is not certain in the way a mathematical-type conclusion can seem to be. Of course, it is reasonable to believe it; but early chronicles and scribes *might* have made a much-copied error; or there may have been a vast conspiracy to deceive.... ? The design argument from regularity, then, is not a knock-down proof; but then it is not reasonable to hope for such a thing. It *may*, if it is a good argument, give some grounds for belief in a designer. At the very least it may show that the ordered character of natures progress makes it *more likely* than it would be if the world was not ordered that way that there is an orderer of power and great intelligence.

When objectors to design arguments say that the central analogy between the order in the physical world and the order in humanly contrived sequences of events is (i) unsound, or (ii) that similar effects do not necessarily imply similar causes, they appear in (i) to be gesturing towards the true point that an analogy is only an analogy and that there *will* be disanalogous features in the comparison between the sides of the analogy which will weaken the argument. To say that the analogy is 'unsound' suggests that the strength of the analogy and of the argument which it supports is a 1 or 0 matter (either there is *conclusive* strength, and the argument is sound, or there is *no* strength, and the argument is *un*sound) when in fact the strength of analogy with the probability of the conclusion are matters of *degree*. The mere existence of some disanalogy, which is inevitable in any analogy, will not of itself render the analogy-argument simply unsound, i.e. worthless.

It is true, with respect to (ii) above that similar effects do not necessarily imply similar causes, if by 'necessarily imply' is meant 'guarantee'. But, once more, in analogy-arguments we are dealing in probabilities: the closer the analogy between the effects which are brought about the more *likely* it is that they had similar causes. So, for example, while the way of carrying out this particular crime (its *modus operandi*) may closely resemble the known and highly distinctive way-of-doing of known criminals from Columbia, that does not 'necessarily imply', i.e. guarantee, that Columbian criminals did it; nevertheless the resemblance makes that conclusion more likely than it would be if there had been no resemblance.

Objectors who criticise design arguments as in (i) and (ii) appear to have misunderstood the nature of arguments by analogy.

Taking further some implications of the above: If this sort of orderedness does make the existence of a designer *more* likely, even if the 'more likely' is only a *little* more likely, this counters one of the (wilder?) statements often made in controversies about God: that there is *no* evidence for God's existence. What is it – what does it mean – for fact f to be *evidence for* proposition p? It means: given that f is a fact, p is more probable than it would have been if f had not been a fact. The fact of regular, patterned sequence in the occurrence of events in nature makes the existence of an immensely intelligent and immensely powerful, omnipresent designer-orderer more probable than it would have been if the world was not ordered but chaotic. Or so this argument says.

The most influential objector to design arguments has been Hume (1711-7). Most of his criticisms have been directed against any version of the design argument. We shall turn to Hume's arguments shortly. But since he himself was challenging that design argument which is based on the order of co-presence, the arrangement together of the parts of a functioning system, like a watch (William Paley's example), we should first see in some more detail what that order and argument are.

People of the 18th and 19th centuries were aware that animals and plants were not only strikingly internally organised to function as they do, their parts adapted to each other in their living systems, but also that they reproduced in their kinds. So the strikingly arranged living things which we encounter come from equally strikingly arranged parents and previous, remoter, ancestors. But where did all this wonderfully arranged life come from? How did such intricately ordered machine-like systems arise? Since they are machine-like in the ingenuity of the arrangement of their parts, there is justification in claiming that they have an origin similar to that of machines which have been contrived by clever human beings. That is, they came about as the result of the intelligent activity of the cosmic ultimate bio-engineer.

Again this is an argument with an analogy as its keystone, and all that was said before about the character of any arguments by analogy applies to this argument. And some of what has been said regarding the argument from the order of succession in time also applies to the order of co-presence, Paley and the watch. For instance, even if it is successful in supporting the conclusion that a divine designer is responsible for the order (of co-presence) which required explanation, it will not support many further beliefs about God which actual religious traditions profess, such as God's being good, forgiving, or having a purpose for the course of human history.

When we turn to assessment of design arguments, very obviously the second sort of argument, from the order of co-presence, (Paley and the watch,) is challenged by the strength of evolutionary doctrine. Charles Darwin (1809 - 1882) and his disciples (such as Richard Dawkins) contend that the kind of order appealed to by this design argument can be accounted for, and should be explained, by the wholly natural process of evolution. Accordingly, they suggest, there is no need to bring a god into the explanation. The true explanation goes rather like this: Amongst the first very simple living organisms formed from the early elements, the early mix and climate which then existed, some had the ability to reproduce; and the process of reproduction gave offspring more or less the same features and attributes as their parent(s). The 'more or less' is important, though. Some (often small) differences from their parent(s) gave a living organism an advantage in its survival prospects in its circumstances, and others (probably most such differences) were disadvantageous. By 'in its circumstances' is meant e.g. the climate, food supplies, the extent of the competition for the necessary food supplies. Over time, circumstances change; accordingly there will be changes concerning which attributes of an organism are advantageous in the struggle for life. Organisms which have, or come to have, disadvantageous attributes will die, in many cases before they can reproduce offspring who would (if they had come to exist) have been likely to inherit their forebears' disadvantaging qualities. Over time, the organisms which are to be found, living and reproducing, will have survival-enhancing qualities. (If they did not they would be less likely to be there at all.) And populations of living things will have the components and attributes and abilities which are suited, functionally effective, in maintaining their life. This can *look* like intelligent design, so say evolutionary theorists like Dawkins, but in reality it is blind nature taking its often blundering, but over the history of life amazing course to produce living things well adapted to function and survive.

So this type of order is brought about not by a sort of super-intelligent designer-watchmaker, but by nature – the Blind Watchmaker. The variations which may, rarely, be great are usually slight (as we see in our own family experience, or in the reproduction of pets or farm animals), and come about by chance. In the long course of the history of life, many types of living creatures have gone out of existence because the set of attributes they had been given from the sequence of inheritance-accidents in their genealogy ill-fitted them to survive for long enough to reproduce. Those which *have* survived, with the consequence that we can admire their design, the functional efficiency of their components – those are the chance outcomes of a chance-determined process. Most biologists regard such a view as resting on very strong evidence.

Before we look at debates about evolution, it is to be noted that the Darwinian-evolutionary explanation of the order of functionally efficient arrangement of parts of living organisms does *not* explain or have any relevance to the other sort of order, that of the patterns of succession among events. That latter sort of order existed even when there were no living things. On lifeless moons and planets, these regularities of succession hold good: e.g. that if liquid water is cooled and cooled, then it solidifies; that unsupported objects move ('fall') to the nearest large mass as gravity determines. The laws of physics express many of these regularities; and the laws of physics appear to apply

27

everywhere. *This* sort of order is, obviously, not explained by Darwinian accounts of how the living creatures we come across have their components arranged in co-operatively functional ways. Darwinian explanations can apply only in the biological sphere.

Controversies rumble on over the Darwinist evolutionary account itself, and it is not possible in the space here to take up most issues. Some which matter for our concerns and require little biological learning are worth a look. Here are two.

First: In Darwin's time the chemical-biological means by which characteristics of parents pass (more, or less) to offspring was not known. In the 20th century, the double helix DNA was identified and described. Now it is understood how, by DNA, offspring usually strongly, if not wholly, resemble ancestors. This discovery fills a gap in Darwinian theory. It helps to explain how variation happens from one generation to the next; and, just as important, it explains how most of the characteristics of one generation are passed on to, retained in, the next. That is vital for persisting survival because it enables the retention over many generations of advantageous developments which have occurred, holding on to gains (and they remain 'gains' for as long as they remain survival-friendly in the conditions). So DNA is essential to the functioning of Darwinian evolution. But DNA is not a simple component. How did *it* come about? The view of those who have examined the question, including Crick one of the discoverers of the structure of DNA, is that, given all we now know about early conditions on our planet, and even if *some* of life's building blocks could have happened by chance in that environment during that time, it is very very improbable that DNA would have happened by chance. The biochemists say that if it did happen like that, it would be a 'miracle'. So, the discovery of DNA, on the one hand helps the Darwinian explanation by making it clearer *how* reproduction of the kind Darwinism needs actually happens. On the other hand, it re-opens debate about the argument from design based on order of co-presence. (Paley's watch hasn't stopped.) How did the earliest DNA, which is a prior condition of any reproduction of living beings, come together? Those who reject or ignore any appeal to an ordering, powerful intelligence, a designer god, offer differing suggestions. Francis Crick's was that simple bacteria may have come through space from somewhere in the universe, carried maybe on asteroids. In this way, life containing DNA may have been seeded on our planet. Lack of evidence about this proposal makes it hard to assess and, for most, hard to believe. Not many do.

Richard Dawkins (see *The Blind Watchmaker* pp.144-5 and more recently *The God Delusion* pp.137f.) reminds us that there are many planets in the universe. And while what we know, taking only our world into account, is that the chance coming-together of DNA is very very unlikely, that unlikeliness may disappear when we take account of the multitude of planets. Even something which has a low probability, and is not likely, on one planet will be a bit more likely to happen in a universe of, say, ten planets. It may actually be rather likely to happen somewhere in a universe of a million planets. And perhaps it has happened in one planet of very many, namely (as it happened) ours. Given a huge number of worlds, Dawkins thinks, the improbability evaporates of DNA's coming together by chance.

We might wonder whether it is reasonable to count most planets in for Dawkins's purpose. In our solar system, only Earth and maybe Mars give even the *very* small chance there is of DNA's coming together. The mere existence of the other planets of the solar system does not make it any more likely that DNA may have happened *somewhere*. Perhaps most planets in the whole universe are like that in that they could *never* bring forth DNA. For all Dawkins says (or can now say?), it may be that far too few planets are likely enough to have hosted DNA to make much difference to the verdict: that its happening to occur somewhere by sheer chance is very unlikely. At present, no one knows what difference Dawkins's appeal to the multitude of planets makes to the likelihood of DNA's chance emergence somewhere.

More than that, suppose that when we are able to consider all the billions of planets it can be reckoned rather likely that DNA did arise by chance somewhere, will that make it more likely than we already reckoned that it happened *here*? Take a parallel: The following is surely very improbable, but not totally impossible: that on this planet and within the same square mile of its surface there once existed at the same time as the result of natural accidents two cubes each measuring 5 metres x 5 metres x 5 metres, one of them composed of pure zinc and the other of pure aluminium. It is surely unreasonable to believe that that ever happened. Now suppose, for argument's sake, that the existence of many planets does make it more probable that a pair of cubes has existed as specified on *some* planet in the universe than it would be if this were the only world. Still, would this appeal to many planets make it *more likely* that the cubes ever existed together and as described earlier, on *our* planet? Surely not? The same sort of reasoning applies in respect of the unlikelihood of DNA's coming about by chance on our planet. The appeal to other worlds does not make it any more reasonable to believe in DNA's chance emergence here than it was reasonable to believe in it before looking for help from 'other worlds'.

To see that from another angle, the procedure Dawkins pursues in referring to the multitude of other planets to argue for the reasonableness of belief in DNA's chance emergence here seems to have this implication: that if there

29

were ten times more planets in the universe than there are, this fact alone would make it more probable than it is (ten times?) that DNA emerged on this planet. Can that be sound reasoning?

The second issue over, in particular, atheistic use of Darwinism concerns sound reasoning. If evolution happened without there being any directing, guiding rational mind controlling it, then we have come about in the following way. Our ancestors, going back as far as we may, were equipped in their environment to *survive* long enough to reproduce; and we are now endowed to *survive* in our conditions. The attributes we have do not prevent us from being alive even if some of them were more useful to our ancestors than to us, and we have merely inherited them; and many of our attributes of course *contribute* to our surviving. But what then of our thinking abilities, especially the ways by which we form beliefs and evaluate them? Why should we suppose that they lead us to the *truth*? Often believing the truth or tending to believe the truth does your survival prospects no good at all. Compare a nervous little furry creature who scuttles for cover whenever a large bird is silhouetted against the sky, falsely believing there is danger when 99 times out of 100 there is none with a bolder mouse which rightly believes that most big birds are not raptors but jackdaws and seagulls. The latter furry animal holds 'truer beliefs', or something of the sort, but its readiness to remain in the open makes it easy prey for the sparrow-hawk which occasionally visits. Tending to have true beliefs is not the same as tending to have beliefs which help survival. If, as Darwinists have claimed, our belief-forming tendencies are for survival, why should we suppose or expect the beliefs we form, and the beliefs we evaluate highly to be *true*? And why should we expect our scientific theories any more than any other of our beliefs to be true? If we are Darwinists, why should we suppose that the Darwinist account of evolution is *true* any more than any of our other beliefs? (See Helm pp.264ff, on this.)

The heyday of that argument from design which focuses on the order of co-presence, the Paley-and-his-watch argument, was the 18th century. Paley's book came out in 1802, but he was drawing on the ideas of many people before him. About a century before Darwin published the *Origin of the Species* (1859), Hume (1711 - 1776) raised objections to design arguments. The design-supporters in Hume's sights were, of course, advocates of that stock 18th century version of design arguments; but much of what Hume said will, if it has force at all, apply to other regular-sequences argument.

He points out (with gusto) how *different* human designing is from what believers would attribute to the deity. Human designers make mistakes, learn, or fail to learn, from them, serve apprenticeships, become too old, are limited in knowledge, skill, and power, have a body, live or die. Perhaps, Hume suggests, when we look around the world and see imperfectly set up and ill functioning systems (e.g. the malfunctioning eyes of the blind) we should conclude that the designer was in his dotage. Often human designing is carried out by teams – shipbuilders or town-planners for instance; perhaps, then, a group of gods designed the systems whose order we notice? The argument by analogy to some sort of design seems to lead to conclusions like these.

On the last point (many 'gods'), there is a principle which says that in trying to explain anything, in science or philosophy, we should not *multiply entities* when there is no need. Appeal to this principle may counter Hume's suggestion here that polytheism is as justified as monotheism. But on the previous points Hume is on stronger ground, certainly as against the order of co-presence, 18th century, argument.

As he is also when he says that God's goodness, God's moral attributes, as these are affirmed by believers, cannot be argued for *from design*. Designers whom we know are morally good and bad, and all points between; their being designers tells us nothing about their *moral* qualities. Hume is correct about this, surely? Supporters of *any* design argument should acknowledge that God's goodness, wisdom, generosity etc. are not to be argued for by appeal to 'design'. (Hume goes further, though. He argues that if we are to be guided by the kind of world we all know around us to belief about the nature of the designer, the appalling unjust suffering in the world is very far from arguing for a just and good designer. This designer, if any, could be nothing of the sort. In this, Hume assumes that there *cannot* be a good purpose in the existence of a world containing pain and sorrow such as our world. Defenders of mainstream theism have said that unless we can *know* that there can be no good, long-term purpose in the history of the universe, we cannot now conclude anything about God's goodness, or moral indifference, or badness. The possibilities for making what is good or great out of this world may be beyond our imagining, so that we cannot make any judgement about its overall merits. And God's character *may* be more fully seen in *particular* events where God makes Godself known definitively at particular times and places. *But* if we are to draw conclusions from generally observed features of the world only, Hume's claims here constitute a serious challenge, at least. (More on this later, in the section on Atheism.)

To argue by analogy, from designed functional systems and their complementary components will, as Hume argues lead us to a God with an all-too human character. This is 'anthropomorphism'.

Design arguments based on the order of succession in time are not only unaffected in strength by evolutionary theorizing, as we saw, but they do *not* lay themselves open to the same (to religious believers) outrageous anthropomorphisms as the functional-arrangement-of-parts argument does. That is because in order to account for the regularities, a being of great-super-human-intelligence, constantly present to the world, immensely powerful, freely acting, but having no body is what is needed. Many of the best-known regularities are described in laws of physics, and many are well known by being familiar in ordinary experience: e.g. water can support your body so that if you jump in you can then swim in it (as you could not do in a less dense liquid, and as you could not be confident of doing if the density of water varied all the time).

To explain the fact that events always succeed one another in these regular and predictable ways, an intelligent being and a being who/which is free (not itself subject to laws of regularity and so its actions determined) is needed. This being's constant and permanent presence to the world is required because these regularities (as described by laws of physics, and other regularities) occur everywhere and at all times, it seems. The power which this being must have is obvious. To have a *body* is for there to be some part of the physical world which you control directly by contrast with other matter, which is not your body and which you can affect if at all only indirectly, by means of your body and possibly other intermediate things. That is, you do not move *your body* by moving something else as you might move a stick. Your body is that matter which you control without controlling anything else more immediately. But the one who orders *all* matter (according to regularities of succession which she/he determines) does so immediately, not by using intermediate matter on some parts of the universe. There is consequently no *distinction* between matter which this being orders directly and that which is only indirectly affected. So there is no chunk of matter which is peculiarly and distinctly under this being's direct control; that is, there is nothing which is its body. If you prefer to say that all matter is, or counts as, the being's body, you may be able to pursue the argument. But even so, this being is no longer being thought of in human terms. Anthropomorphism, which from the stand point of most believers undermines the design argument from the adaptedness to purpose of the parts of functioning systems like watches – anthropomorphism is much reduced when order of regularity of succession is the basis for the argument from order/design.

For that reason and because it is unaffected by Darwinian arguments, the appeal to the regularity of succession among events in time is thought to give the best prospect for a worthwhile design argument.

Two more of Hume's objections need to be considered: the first concerns the origin of a designer and/or the design, while the second says an analogy-argument is ruled out because the universe is unique.

So the first asks how, if we accept the need for a divine designer, we can explain the *designer's* existence: how did (s)he come to exist? Hume apparently assumes that if no explanation for the designer's existing is provided then the explanation of order by appealing to a designer fails. But this is an uncalled for assumption. A biologist may explain the discovery of some bones by saying that a rare kind of dinosaur existed in that region. And that will be a genuine explanation of the bones even if he cannot explain how dinosaurs or a dinosaur *came* to be there. So for an intelligent designer's activity to account for order in the world it is *not* necessary further to explain how the designer came to exist.

Hume also asks how, if, there is a designer, the *design* came to exist. If the order of the world requires that there has been a designer with a sort of plan or blueprint of the universe where did the *plan* come from? However, if the intelligent designer is creative, as good designers are, bringing ideas and plans into existence (rather as poets and novelists invent poems and stories) and then making actual what was planned, we have no need to ask further where the plan came from. The designer invented it out of the designer's original creativity.

Can we argue by analogy about something, in this case the universe, which is the *only* thing of its kind? Hume claims that we cannot argue by analogy about the existence of a universe which is the only one of its kind, the only universe we can know. While it is true that analogy argument requires comparison, and that we cannot compare the universe and its coming-to-be with the emergence of any other *universe*, we can usefully compare it and what makes it up with other ordered sequences or systems devised by human designers. Described as 'the Universe', the universe is the only one of its kind we know, or can know. But as an ordered system, or containing ordered systems, it *can* be compared to other ordered systems; and conclusions can be properly drawn about it origins. (Uniqueness is relative to description. As: being the only son of Mr & Mrs Jones of 53 High Street, Elgin, Jack is unique but as: having a pumping heart he is not unique.)

For a further much admired presentation of an argument from design, see Richard Taylor's introductory book *Metaphysics*, the chapter on 'God' (Chap. 7).

During the 20th century, a number of scientific discoveries led to the construction of **'anthropic' arguments** for God's existence. Like members of a family they resemble one another, yet with some differences. The resemblance is this: They all note that for conscious life to arise, and so for there to be persons such as ourselves capable of thought and love, many of the physical constants of the universe had to be almost exactly as each one of them is, and all together. Examples of these constants are the electrical charge of the proton (which is one of the basic particles of matter), the mass of the proton, the speed of light, the gravitational constant, and Planck's constant. For our purposes, what we are asked to grasp is just that these are basic facts about our material world; they determine the rate of expansion of the universe and the possibility of there being stars and planets. More than that, and to quote B.J. Carr and M.J. Rees, in *Nature* 1979, 'the possibility of life as we know it evolving in the universe depends on the value of a few basic physical constants – and is in some respects remarkably sensitive to their numerical values'. If gravity were stronger stars would die young before humanoid life could evolve. And similar things can be said with respect to other of the constants. (This is not controversial or eccentric. Rees was Astronomer Royal, Professor of Astrophysics at Cambridge University and President of the Royal Society.) Intelligent humanoid life could have evolved only in a universe like this, i.e. like this within a very narrow range of values of the constants. John Leslie (see Helm pp.273ff.) calls this joint occurrence of the large range of basic physical constants which are necessary conditions for intelligent life, 'Fine Tuning'. Not only is all this widely agreed amongst astronomers and physicists, but its improbability is agreed also: it is agreed to be hugely improbable.

Earlier versions of the anthropic argument such as that of F.R. Tennant did not attempt to provide an estimate in figures of the unlikeliness that the precise conditions for the emergence of life would come together. His argument was just that the action of a divine designer gives the best explanation for its having actually happened. Physics and astrophysics since then enable quantified estimates of improbability to be made. Princeton physics professor D.N. Page estimated that the odds against our universe's being 'fine tuned' as it is are one in many billions. Writers such as Leslie have drawn the conclusion that it is reasonable to affirm the existence of a divine creating intelligence.

Others have resisted that conclusion while not disputing the striking fact of 'fine tuning'. One objection to the creating-intelligence explanation is that there are, or may be, many billions of universes, so many that (at least) *one* was likely to be rather as ours is. And ours, of course, is that one. The many-universes theory is itself controversial. There can hardly be *evidence* for other universes, although there is a much disputed multiple-universe interpretation of recent theorizing in physics. (Another universe has to be in a different space and time from ours; if it is not, then it is part of this universe. And how can there be available to us *evidence* from another space and time?) If the only or main reason for proposing the many worlds view is that it can explain fine-tuning, and the contest to explain fine-tuning lies between the many-worlds view and a god, the outcome of the contest should depend on which of these explanations also accounts for *other* things.

34

Leslie thinks that the existence of a designer god would also explain why there are laws of nature, worthy of the name 'laws' at all. Accordingly, *he* favours belief in God as the explanation of fine-tuning. A person might quite possibly reckon that a god's existence would account for yet other facts (such as the human ability to recognise logical or mathematical truths, seen by the 'eye' if the mind rather than the eyes in your head) whereas many-universe theories will not; such a person will at least think it likelier that there is a god. The reasonableness of this conclusion will depend on whether God is *needed* to explain such other factors, and whether God *does* explain them.

Atheism

Atheism in the strict sense is the proposition that there is no god. In this section, we are to look at atheism in this strict sense, and more particularly the *grounds* which have been given for holding their belief by atheistic thinkers.

Down the centuries, 'atheist' has also and often been applied comparatively loosely to people whose views and practices clearly departed from the generally accepted, established religion of that society at that time. Even though they did not actually deny the existence of a god, their view was called atheistic. It was a term of disapproval applied to religious and moral dissidents. Some such dissidents were defiantly content to be called 'atheist'. Bertrand Russell saw no good reason to think that there is a god; but it is not clear that he was an atheist in the strict sense.

In order to establish that there is no god, it is not sufficient to reason that all known arguments *for* the existence of a god are inadequate, invalid or weak. Even if that can be successfully done, it will *only* show that a god's existence is not indicated by *these* arguments. Perhaps there may be others which are sound. Perhaps new evidence will emerge (as supporters of the theistic argument from 'fine-tuning' claim has happened in the last few decades) which will justify or compel belief in a god. Perhaps there is a god, but no strong evidence or argument to make belief in God's existence reasonable for us. (Perhaps there are no sound arguments either for the existence of a god or against the existence of a god and *agnosticism* is the only reasonable view: not knowing.) Rational atheism then requires to go beyond destruction of arguments *for* a god's existence. Atheism has to present reasons for believing that there *is* no god. If any of these is a good reason there will be a *ground* for atheism.

There are two ways in which there may be grounds for atheism, and atheists have appealed to each of these. The first does not give evidence or logical deductions in order to show that atheism is *true*. Rather it offers reasons for adopting an attitude of atheism, reasons for assenting to atheism whether we can demonstrate its truth or not. Often we do adopt a view for reasons other than our knowing it to be true. The coach tells us that we can beat this previously unbeaten team and we try to believe him, and may possibly believe him even though he offers no evidence for what he says, because to have that belief helps our chances in the match ahead. Or we may, as a matter of policy, believe the best of people when their actions are ambiguous: they may be well-motivated or ill-motivated so far as the evidence goes, but we think the best of them. So this first kind of justification of atheism does not give evidence or logical inferences to show that atheism is true; rather we should adopt it and hold to it as a matter of good practice. The second sort of argument for atheism does present arguments for atheism's truth. As we shall see there are arguments which are purely about logic, while others appeal to evidence.

But first, to atheists who have recommended atheistic belief as a matter of good practice: The influential essay of W.K. Clifford (Helm pp.238ff.) argues that all the beliefs we have can, and often will, affect our actions, our dealings with other people and the kinds of differences we make to our world. Accordingly we should take responsibility and care over what we believe, for our sakes and especially (as Clifford appears to think) for the sake of others: so we should be scrupulous to believe only what we are bound to believe on the evidence before us. Since religious beliefs do and should make a significant difference to how we behave and what we say, religious beliefs seem to fall squarely under Clifford's concern; and many writers since Clifford have taken him to have religion much in mind in framing his principle, which says that it is wrong always, everywhere and for anyone to believe anything on insufficient evidence.

Clifford's principle is employed by many writers who argue against a belief that there is a god on the ground that there is insufficient evidence to justify that belief. Whether you think that is so will depend on your view of the arguments discussed earlier in the course, and of other arguments for God's existence. Here it needs to be noted again that even if there is insufficient known evidence for God's existence, it may not follow that atheism should be adopted. If there is insufficient ground (evidence or pure reasoning) to establish the truth of atheism either, then the reasonable view to hold about God's existence is, on Clifford's maxim, that we do not have a proper basis for belief one way or the other whether God exists. This would be **agnosticism**.

Clifford's concern is about the effects which false beliefs can have in misdirecting the activities of individuals and mis-shaping society-so that harm ensues or good is thwarted. Accordingly, a Cliffordian atheist might argue that atheistic belief will, more firmly than agnosticism, prevent unfounded belief in God, and will head off all the harms which belief in God can bring – such as time-wasting worship, or the practice of humility, or indoctrination. Atheistic conviction will also resolve a paralysing uncertainty which agnosticism can generate, and free people to think and act well, unconstrained by religious anxieties or propaganda. That way of recommending atheism will only carry weight with people who already agree that belief in God *does* have these implications for human practice, and that they *are* undesirable or harmful, so the argument will appeal to already convinced secularists. *They* may even think that it is convincing. But if a person still has an open mind, or suspects that the practices which belief in God calls for may be very desirable, this sort of reason for being an atheist will be worthless.

Flew introduced the concept of a *presumption* (see Helm, pp.336ff.) in order to argue that a lack of evidence for God's existence does justify the adoption of atheism. A presumption is more than an assumption (which would be something like a belief which is not, or not now, supported as true by reasons or argument). A presumption in this context, as also in e.g. the law courts, is adopted because to adopt it is a valuable part of our *procedure* in order to carry out our particular purpose. In the law courts in this and other countries, it is fundamental to *this* purpose: to avoid convicting innocent people. The presumption we're thinking about now is the *presumption of innocence*. The prosecution must make and sustain a convincing case that the accused person is guilty before the court can convict. Until that prosecution case has been made and sustained in argument (with the defence) the accused is presumed to be innocent. This presumption of innocence shapes the procedure, whose purpose involves convicting the guilty – but *only* the guilty. (Flew could add this: It is often very hard for a person to present a good case that *they* did *not* commit a particular crime which is alleged to have been committed; and if an accused had to present evidence and argue for her/his innocence, from scratch, and not simply answer the case and deal with the evidence presented by the prosecution, many (more) innocent people would be convicted.) But priority is in fact given to avoiding convicting the innocent, so innocence is presumed unless and until a strong prosecution case convinces the court. What, then, is the purpose prompting Flew to advocate a presumption of *atheism*?

It is that if anyone is to establish and properly to claim to *know* that there is a god, that person must have grounds, justification. You can *believe*, not very respectably and maybe foolishly, without any grounds or reasons. If I believe that Mr McCall is a healer while admitting that I have no reason to believe that, I really do have the belief, however silly I am. And it may *happen* to be a true belief, or it may not. But if I don't have grounds or evidence it is not *knowledge*. It is not established. If we are to *know* that God exists, then not only must God actually exist, but we must have sufficient reasons or evidence for God's existence. Until that case (reasons or evidence) is forthcoming, we do not *know*, we have not established God's existence. Flew says, 'in that situation the only reasonable posture must be that of either the negative atheist or agnostic.' Until the case for God's existence is well made, he urges, this posture should be our presumption.

Flew called the book in which he argued as above *The Presumption of Atheism*. It is easy to see from what he says why before any argument or debate about God's existence has begun, an attitude of neutrality, a provisional agnosticism will be appropriate while we await the presentation of a case. But why adopt the presumption of *atheism* in the absence of any case for atheism? Why is the burden of making out a case not *equally* on theist and atheist before either of their views is evaluated and adopted? Flew told us that presumptions are to be adopted to serve our purposes / priorities as when we adopt the presumption of innocence to avoid the conviction of innocent people. True, to have *knowledge* about something, for something to *be* knowledge requires that there be good grounds, justification; but that applies to knowledge of theism and atheism alike / equally, surely? A presumption in favour of *atheism* must, it seems, serve someone's purpose and priorities. The purpose specified by Flew, to acquire well-founded *knowledge*, does not favour a presumption of atheism over theism: to be known, *both* need grounds. Can it be that it is (or was) more important in Flew's eyes to avoid believing in God if there is no God than it is to avoid unbelief if there is in fact a god? A preference of *that* sort may have a rational basis, as yet undisclosed to us, it may, though, reflect an emotional preference, whether or not it is recognised as such. Or again, sometimes people who have a view which they think many or most others share are inclined to assume that this view is the neutral view, putting the requirement to make a case on anyone who disagrees. The general view is the default view! It would be unworthy of Flew for that to be true of him here. His presumption of atheism seems, though, to be at least open to question.

38

Note: Flew is no longer an atheist or agnostic, having come to accept that there is enough evidence for a god. But he may well still hold that (in the absence of any such evidence) there is a presumption of atheism.

Should Clifford's principle which has been so widely used to try to justify agnosticism or atheism, be accepted? Are there beliefs which are rationally held but which do not rest on evidence or argument? It seems at least not quite appropriate, if you are looking at what is very obviously a tomato, to say that you have *evidence* that there is a tomato. You don't 'have evidence', surely? You just see it. Perhaps, some have said, awareness and knowledge of God are like that if a person can have experience of God on an analogy with seeing or hearing (see Helm, pp.366ff. for Alston's contribution, saying this sort of thing).

What is more, if you do have to have the support of enough evidence for anything you justifiably believe, there is a problem. Suppose you believe something, call it S, and you have evidence T which you also believe, in support of S; since you believe T, in order to be justified in that, you must have evidence for *it*, which you believe, call that evidence U. To believe U rationally by Cliffordian lights you need evidence for U, and evidence for that evidence, and so on. If you must have evidence for all that you believe responsibly, how can the required series of beliefs ever come to a foundation, a solid starting point? How will we ever come to believe anything properly?

In fact, there are beliefs which we all treat as reasonable, but for which it is not *possible* to have evidence. We all treat past experience as a reliable guide to what will happen. We learn by experience that fire burns and hurts. Because we have noticed that fire has generally burned or hurt those who touch it, we reason that this fire and to-morrow's fire will do likewise. But what grounds have we for treating past experience as a guide to what will happen, what *evidence*? Evidence would have to be from the past. But to use evidence from the past as a reason for holding that past experience *is* a guide to what will happen is to assume what is in question: to use this evidence requires us to *assume* that our past experience is a good guide to the future which is what is in question. (Hume is a prominent philosopher who made this point.) But even though we cannot have evidence for it, the belief that past experience is a guide to what will happen is surely a rational belief. The general reliability of *memory* is also believed in, reasonably enough surely? We take it that memory provides (though not infallibly) access to what happened in the past. You remember having coffee for breakfast, or if you are not sure about *that* you probably remember that you did *have* breakfast; and you take the experience of remembering reliably to re-present the past. Memory recalls the past, we believe. But what evidence can there be for *this*? Any evidence we try to use has to *assume* that memory is reliable, because to test the reliability of any particular memory you need to rely on other memories. Suppose you wonder whether you did have coffee at breakfast, as (you think) you remember doing. You look at the coffee jar you bought yesterday to see if it has been opened, into the dishwasher to see if your cup is there with coffee stains.......For any of that to help, though, you need to *remember* that you bought *that* coffee jar and which cup is yours and whether you used it today. Our relying on our memory in relation to some event cannot be justified by evidence which does not itself depend on reliable memory. Old newspapers? You need to *remember* what features of the supposedly remembered event identify it, especially, maybe, its date. So here is another rationally held belief, in the reliability of memory, which does not and seemingly cannot depend on evidence.

Whether Clifford's principle can be defended against these difficulties, and if it has to be replaced then replaced with what, are large questions. People who appeal to Clifford's principle to support atheism or agnosticism about God appear to be superficial at best.

We move next to arguments for atheism, not merely for a procedural presumption to be adopted that atheism (or perhaps agnosticism) be taken as true, but to show that in fact there is no god.

The first says that the very concept of god is incoherent; not only is there no god, but there *cannot* exist such a being as most believers describe and identify as God. The concept of god is said to be like that of a colourless yellow ball, or the largest even number: nothing *can* fit these specifications. One such problem about the concept of god arises because God is said to be essentially all-powerful or omnipotent; nothing will *be* God unless it is all-powerful. But now omnipotence is argued to be impossible. Why? As a preliminary to the debate, it is generally accepted that God, even an omnipotent god, cannot be expected to do anything which is *logically* impossible, like making an oval square; but that *that* will not make God less than omnipotent. Try to think of this thing (making an oval square) which God cannot do, the state of affairs (there being an oval square) which God cannot bring about. What would it *be* for there to be an oval square? No state of affairs could be a state of affairs in which there is an oval square; God's 'inability' to create an oval square comes not from a lack of power on God's part because no power whatever, even infinite power, *could* bring about an oval square. (If you cannot draw a square properly, that is due to a lack of ability or power; but it is not due to lack of ability or power that you cannot draw an oval square.) The expression 'the existence of an oval square' does not specify a state of affairs at all, in fact; and it may mislead if we call it an 'impossible state of affairs' as if this state of things might somehow exist if only it could be managed, but it can't. God cannot bring it about not because of an overwhelming difficulty in doing so but because there being an oval square does not specify any state of affairs. Nor does 'there being a planet with fewer than zero moons'. It is no slur on God's power that God cannot bring about such *pseudo*-situations. There is wide agreement on that.

An all-powerful being will, however, surely have to be able to accomplish anything that is logically possible. Yet there *seem* to be logically possible, not pseudo, states of affairs which God cannot bring about where we do know what it would be for *these* states of affairs to exist. Here is one example which is given in order to argue for atheism: The idea of someone's making something which she cannot then destroy makes sense. People sometimes do it. Take a boulder as an example. The idea of an indestructible boulder makes sense. Can God make a boulder which God cannot then destroy? If God cannot do *that* then surely God is not all powerful. But if God *can* do that, then God has created a boulder which even God cannot destroy; so since God cannot destroy the boulder, *this* is something which God cannot do, and, again, God is not all-powerful. Hence, it is argued, the supposedly essential attribute of God, God's omnipotence is impossible.

These two lines of response have been offered (among others): The first (i) aims to counter the argument and deal with the alleged problem for the concept of omnipotence in God; the second (ii) concedes that omnipotence even in its more exactly defined form (ability to bring about genuine, rather than pseudo, states of affairs) cannot be attributed to God, and that God should be called Almighty instead.

(i) Defenders of omnipotence (see the article by Mavrodes, pp.112-5 in the volume of readings eds. Peterson, Hasker, etc.) argue that the believer in God who says that God is omnipotent (i.e. can bring about any non-pseudo state of affairs) should also say that the *omnipotent* God's bringing about an indestructible thing is a pseudo state of affairs: it is logically impossible for God to bring it about that *God* should create an indestructible anything. If God is all-powerful then there cannot be a logically possible, non-pseudo, situation in which God could not destroy a boulder. In asking for God, the all powerful God, to be able to create an *indestructible* object the advocate of atheism is asking for a pseudo, logically impossible, state of affairs. It is therefore that atheistic critic who is guilty of incoherence rather than the believer in an omnipotent god. Debate continues.

(ii) This response suggests that believers should say (as many of the Creeds have said) that God is almighty, rather than that God is omnipotent or all-powerful with the difficulties of definition and coherence which we have discussed. God's almighty-ness is said to mean: that God is the source of all power for whom there is no frustration or failure. God can and does all that God wishes or purposes. (Probably this does not include making indestructible boulders.) This account of God's power is more in keeping with the faiths of Jewish, Christian and Islamic believers (who think of God as having acted and as acting towards us in specific ways) without raising the philosophical issues we have studied above.

The contention that the very concept of god contains attributes that make God impossible has also focused on other attributes than omnipotence. We have space to turn to only one: omniscience, Gods' knowing everything. Here the problem is not the *internal* coherence of the concept of god, but the compatibility of God's knowledge with this strongly held conviction: If we believe that we have *free will* in choosing to do this thing rather than that, as most of us probably do believe, how is *that* compatible with God's knowing everything, and in particular, God's knowing before you act what you will do? Suppose you decided to have a bridie at lunch yesterday, and to buy it at Bingley's the Baker; and suppose that that is what you did. If God knows everything, then God has always known your choice and action in this bridie-buying. So God knew, say last year, that you would buy Bingley's bridie yesterday. Now if God knew that you would do that, then it was necessary that you would do that. (If you had done something else, say done without lunch, God could *not* have *known* that you would buy Bingley's bridie.) If, since God knew you would, you necessarily bought the bridie, then your action was not free; it was done necessarily. And what's true of that action will be true of all our actions – since God foreknew them all, if God knows everything. It seems that we have to choose between our freedom and God's omniscience. If you are very sure of our freedom you will say there can *be* no omniscient being. In this way then God's omniscience raises a question over whether there can be an all-knowing God. (See Peterson and Hasker: Pike on 'Divine Omniscience and Voluntary Action' pp.149ff.)

Many believers in God (Jewish, Christian and Islamic) have found no great difficulty here because they have accepted that we have no freedom. They believe this, usually, for more reasons than only the omniscient foreknowledge of God; but that has been one reason (e.g. of the American philosopher-theologian Jonathan Edwards). For these people the problem is solved.

Those who believe in human freedom have either attacked the conception of God as all-knowing or attempted to show that our freedom is compatible with divine omniscience. Since it is doubtful if a being of *limited* knowledge could be *God*, the attack on the conception of God-as-all-knowing is one way of supporting atheism.

One response to the problem is to say that God is not in time, and so even if God does know everything, God does not have *fore* knowledge. God's knowledge is timeless, on this view: God, in God's timeless eternity, is aware of all that happens in the history of the universe. God knows that these events are past, present or future to us; but God exists out of, 'above', our time series, in God's eternal present. A problem which has been raised for this proposed solution has been that it seems to entail God thinks e.g. the death of Ceasar, the Battle of Bannockburn, and D-Day 1944 happened at the same time, i.e. God's eternal present. Perhaps the distinction between our time, in which there's past, present and a future, of which God is aware and God's eternal present deals with that: God knows that for *us* there are before and after. But the very idea of an eternal present is difficult to grasp. It is hard enough to know what the ordinary present, in time, may be: does it disappear between past and future? 'The whole of eternity in God's present' calls for analysis, at least. (See Peterson, Hasker etc., Boethius 'God is Timeless' pp.155ff.)

Turning to another response to the problem of divine foreknowledge and creatures' freedom, we can gain some better understanding of the issues, and perhaps, see that there is *something* wrong with the move from foreknowledge to the elimination of freedom. The 'necessity' which follows from God's foreknowledge, for example, your action, comes from the nature of knowledge. If anyone *knows* anything A, then *necessarily* A is true. If A is not true, then it cannot be *known*. It may merely be believed, even though it isn't true. It is the logic of the concept of knowledge, what it is to *know*, that leads to the necessity which is at the heart of the matter.

Now the problem seems to apply to knowledge of *past* actions as well as future ones. If you *know* that World War I came to an end in 1918, then *necessarily* it did end in 1918; so the reasoning goes. But does not this conclusion seem more dubious? Can your knowing about them *now* entail that events in 1918 were necessary, *had* to occur as they did? Carrying this further, suppose a man Jackson in 1900 accidentally killed someone Johnson, without Jackson's realising what he'd done. He fired a shot at what he thought was a boar and unknown to him hit someone hiding from justice in the thick forest. The human remains were discovered a century later, and you, a forensic pathologist and local historian, worked out what happened. Until you tell someone only you know, or have ever known who killed the victim and how it happened. And suppose for the moment that there is no all-knowing god. You (alone) now *know* that Jackson killed Johnson, so, necessarily Jackson killing Johnson: this was something that had to happen. That is implausible enough. But are we to say, further, that until you figured it out, it was not necessary that Jackson killed Johnson (the death might have been avoided) whereas it became necessary once you came to know it? How could your *coming* to know it take away the freedom of action of Jackson and Johnson and the accidental nature of the death? That seems ridiculous. What is clear is that we have a problem over how to think properly about knowledge, necessity and freedom; but that something seems wrong about the pattern of argument which appeared to show God's omniscience incompatible with creatures' freedom.

We move now from these attempts to show that essential divine attributes are either internally incoherent or incompatible with other belief, which we are confident about, to another sort of familiar argument for atheism: the **Problem of Evil**. This argument draws attention to the way the world observably is. It argues that if God is essentially all-powerful and altogether good or loving, the evils we see cannot exist. Since they do exist, any cosmic power there may be, if any, cannot be both all powerful and altogether good, cannot be God. This is the argument for atheism.

More fully, the argument runs like this: If there is a god who is all-powerful, and altogether good and loving, this god will be able, by divine power, to exclude all evils from the world; and in view of God's goodness and love God will wish and purpose to do so. But there *are* evils such as the sufferings which afflict so many people, and in ways unrelated to their deserving: The suffering of small babies, famines, diseases, war, earthquakes, tsunamis .... So, there is no god.

It is hard to deny that there are evils. Those who have tried to maintain that evil is an *illusion*, or that belief in the existence of evils is a *mistake* which right thinking might eliminate, have to face the point that illusions and mistakes are evils of a kind too. So at least those evils have to be reckoned with. (In any case Jewish, Christian and Islamic believers insist that there *is* a great deal that is evil in the world. Redemption, salvation, forgiveness, obedience, transformation are the sorts of concepts in which they deal, and these imply that there is something wrong, to be put right, about the world. It is not open to them to deny that there are evils, even if it ever occurred to them to do so.)

Atheists who argue in favour of their atheism from the fact(s) of evil commonly contend that as a matter of *logic* the existence of evil is incompatible with the existence of an all-powerful, all-loving god. You cannot reasonably accept that there are evils *and* that there is such a god. (See e.g. Peterson, Hasker, etc. pp.304ff., J.L. Mackie's view) It is, on this view, *impossible* that there can be a god of this kind, and evil(s).

If this argument for atheism is to be defeated, its critic will have to show that it *is* possible that this god of power and love co-exists with evil. The critic does not have to show that what she argues to be *possible* is also, in fact, the *actual* state of affairs in order to undermine the claim to logical rigour made by the atheist. If there is a possible scenario in which evils may be compatible with the existence of God, this atheistic argument in logic fails.

One line of criticism, sketching a possible scenario of that sort has been (what is called) the *Freewill Defence*. This disputes that step in the atheist's reasoning which says that if God is wholly good/loving, then God will wish to exclude all evils from the world. This is because some evils may be necessary for the existence of very great goods (and the evils are a price worth paying for the sake of such goods). We are not talking here about evils which God's *power* could enable God to exclude while securing the good in question. (Compare the case of a surgeon who may only be able to save your life by amputating your arm whereas the great god could save you by use of God's power, without amputations.) There may be evils which are *necessary* for securing certain goods, even by an all powerful being: for example heroic mutual support is possible only where there are great dangers or needs or hardships. Even an all-powerful being could not enable there to be *this* good without these evils.

In response to the problem of evil, the Freewill Defence says that in order to open up the possibility of certain very great goods even an all-powerful god must at least *risk* evils, even great evils. The very great goods include love, moral growth and moral goodness. Unless God's creatures have *freedom*, it is said, loving relations between them, and any moral qualities are impossible. You have to be free to enter loving personal relations. A robot can neither have a love-life, nor love its neighbour as itself. But if creatures have genuine freedom, they may misuse it, to act and develop in evil ways. So, to open up these goods God has taken the risk of evils, and evils have followed. They have followed not because God's goodness is lacking but because risking these evils was essential if the great goods are to be possible. Note that the modern Freewill Defender does not claim or need to be arguing that this is how evils have actually come about, or that God *did* take the risk of the evils to make the goods possible. All that is needed to undermine the atheist's case is that God's taking the risk, etc., is a coherent possibility. And if this is even a possible scenario, the logical force of the atheist's argument is taken away: we cannot rigorously deduce from the existence of evils that there is no god.

Not all evils can obviously be accounted for as in the Freewill Defence set out so far. Wars, cruelty and murder may be accounted for that way. But what about earthquakes or epidemics? These are instances of what are called natural evils, as distinct from the evils brought about by the misuse of human freedom (which are often called moral evils). The existence of these evils does not obviously fit in to the Freewill Defences account so far: They do not always or generally seem to be ways by which there can arise goods so great as to outweigh the evils. Certainly these natural disasters can call forth generosity, sacrificial bravery, sympathy and other praiseworthy responses, but it can hardly be claimed with much confidence that the goods outweigh the evils. (Any calculation or weighing-up here is difficult, at best.) The Freewill Defender commonly, at this point, says it is possible that there are immensely powerful non-human creatures of God, to whom freedom has been given for the same good reason that freedom is given to us. And if there are such beings it is possible that one or more of them has misused that freedom and brings about the disasters we call natural disasters in our world. We may have little other reason to believe in such malevolent creatures; but the important point is that their existence is *possible*. This mere possibility is what is said to reveal the atheist's reasoning as flawed: her logic is not rigorous because all the evils which there are may be compatible with God's good and loving will.

One response to the Freewill Defence is that of Mackie and others. They say that a god could have created creatures such that these creatures would always choose rightly and well, while still choosing freely. A powerful and good god would surely have done that. God would have determined creatures' choices, but they *would* be free choices in that if a creature *had* chosen differently from the way in which she was made to choose, she could have done so, there would have been no external constraint preventing her. A controversy emerges at this point over what counts as *freedom* here, and whether Mackie's sort of freedom *does* open up the goods for the sake of which (so the Freewill Defence says) God might have given freedom.

Another, rather different response to the Freewill Defence says that it supports a Stoic rather than a Jewish, Christian or Islamic view of God and of creatures' relation to God. Suppose that the Freewill Defence is accepted. We then have a conception in which the cosmic mind or God has set up a system. In this system there are many free creatures, so that love and goodness can emerge and flourish; some creatures misuse their freedom with the result that there is immense harm and suffering for very many. What is the advocate of this Freewill Defence saying to people who suffer grievously?

That she/he should recognise (maybe even admire) the good purpose being fulfilled in this system which God in God's wisdom has created; the terrible sufferings borne by people are to be regarded as a cost regrettably incurred in the operation of the system. The Stoic in classical times urged everyone to admire the wonderful ingenious system of nature and bear whatever pains come to them in the course of events, recognizing that the system's wondrous operation entailed those pains. (Peterson, Hasker, etc. contains Adams 'Horrendous Evils ....' pp.365ff.)

Jews, Christians and Islamic believers hold that God values and cares about the deepest welfare of each individual among God's people. For them, God is *not* merely the originator of an ingenious and admirable system which individuals serve as parts, so that if they suffer they are to see themselves as casualties of what is still a system to be admired. But the Freewill Defence does not make room for belief in a god whose individual creatures are God's concern. The nature and distribution of evils in the world may perhaps be fitted into a rather Stoic view along the lines of the Freewill Defence. But as it stands the Freewill Defence fails to explain how belief in a loving god who has a good purpose and care for his individual people is compatible with the world we see, its cruel hardships and seemingly pointless suffering? That is the question still confronting the religious traditions indicated at the beginning of this paragraph.

Believers from these traditions may firstly point out how easy it is to *say* that God could and should have brought about a world in which such and such a kind of thing does not happen. God, we may say, could have accomplished God's purposes without the Boxing Day tsunami, without there being diseases, without our dog's being run over. He could, at least, have made us so that we hurt less. But in urging these things, what sort of world are people requiring? Clearly it would have to be a different sort of world. Are we wanting the suspension of the normal order of nature (the recurring sequences of ordered successions of events)? The consequent unpredictability among events could make purposive action impossible, and the breakdown of any order seems to await at the end of that train of thought. Again, do we want there to be no such things as, for instance, tsunamis? If that is not to be achieved by the blocking of natural laws, are we looking for a world with no sea? Or no tectonic plates of the earth's crust shifting as they do? We will have to have a redesigned world, perhaps the universe. *Perhaps*, if we were a lot more competent in making judgements about such cosmic possibilities we would find that it is hard to devise a world which would be better than this. Perhaps, for all we can say with any reasonable confidence the choices are: this world (or a world very like it), a world less good for the welfare of its inhabitants, or no world at all? It is not just obvious that a world without this or that source of pain, without tragedy could be made without there being a large cost in some other way. Confident conviction that God could have done better, calls for a fuller, thought-through specification of the alternative design.

Particular religious traditions will have their own *distinctive* understandings of evils. Christians contend that to a world where tragedy, pain and injustice are abundant, God has come, sharing and participating as a victim in the tragedy, pain and injustice, and giving Godself to be known. God has, it is said, come out of love for creatures and God intends that they should love God too. If, as Christians hold, knowing and loving God is the greatest of goods, and if we now know God most closely in suffering – knowing God in Christ by our identifying with him as he with us, in suffering, e.g. in prayer–devotion, in the bread and wine which is his body and blood – we may be able rationally enough to say something like this: 'Although we do not know enough to know why the world has to involve horrific suffering and tragedy, we meet God in it and have an assurance (as from a loving parent to a confused and suffering child) that all will be well.'

(Jewish and Islamic believers have also pointed to ways in which, notwithstanding our limited grasp of the possibilities open to an all-powerful god, we can see how this god may have had good purposes in the world we know.)

Whether anyone is entitled to assert such things will depend on e.g. what good reasons there are for believing that there is such a person as God who *was* in Christ, and that we can know God now. It is beyond the scope of this booklet to discuss these last two points. But if these things are *possible*, the problem of evil, given acknowledged human limitations, can perhaps be lived with by believers? That is what they say. The Problem of Evil is not thereby solved, if being 'solved' means our having a good explanation of just why the all-powerful, all loving god allows, and even shares in, the consequences of evil. To do that, it seems, we would need a much wider and deeper grasp of the possibilities than we do have.